THIS BOOK BELONGS
TO:

_____

Copyright Page:
Big Questions for Little Geniuses: What is Coding?
Written, Designed & Illustrated by GiggleTree Publishing
Copyright © 2025 GiggleTree Publishing. All rights reserved. No part of this book may be reproduced, stored in a retrieval system, or transmitted in any form or by any means, electronic, mechanical, photocopying, recording, or otherwise, without the prior written permission of the publisher, except in the case of brief quotations embodied in critical reviews and certain other noncommercial uses permitted by copyright law.

For permissions or inquiries, please contact:
hello@giggletreepublishing.com
First Edition
ISBN: 978-1-0683529-3-5

Disclaimer:
The information provided in What Is Coding? A Kids' Guide to Computers and Programming is for educational purposes only. While every effort has been made to ensure accuracy, coding and technology evolve rapidly, and some details may become outdated. This book does not provide professional advice, certification, or guarantee any specific outcomes from coding practices.
The authors, publisher, and associated parties are not responsible for any errors, omissions, or outcomes resulting from the use of this book. By using this book, readers agree that the authors and publisher shall not be held liable for any direct, indirect, incidental, or consequential damages, including but not limited to data loss, security breaches, or technical issues arising from the application of the content.
Parents, guardians, and educators are encouraged to supervise children's online activities and ensure safe and responsible use of technology. This book does not endorse or promote any specific software, platform, or third-party services.
By purchasing and using this book, you agree to indemnify and hold harmless the authors, publisher, and affiliates from any claims, liabilities, damages, or expenses arising from its use.

Introduction

Welcome to What Is Coding?, an exciting journey into how we use computers to create, solve problems, and bring ideas to life.

Have you ever wondered how video games are made, how websites work, or how robots follow instructions? The answer is coding, the language that tells computers what to do.

In this book, we'll explore what coding is, how programmers think, and why computers need clear instructions to work properly. We'll dive into different types of coding, from building apps to creating animations, and discover how coding shapes the world around us.

But don't worry, you don't need to be a computer expert to understand it. This book breaks everything down in a fun and easy way, with real-world examples, surprising facts, and cool activities to help you think like a coder.

So, are you ready to unlock the power of coding? Let's get started!

BIG QUESTIONS FOR LITTLE GENIUSES

WHAT IS CODING?

A KIDS' GUIDE TO CREATING WITH COMPUTERS

Table of Contents

① What is coding?....................................8

② How do computers understand code?...16

③ What are programming languages?..24

④ How do coders write code?................30

⑤ What can you do with code?..............37

⑥ How do video games use coding?.......45

⑦ How do websites and apps work?.......52

⑧ What is the future of coding?.............60

⑨ How can YOU start coding?................65

⑩ Extras: Glossary...................................71

What is coding?

Imagine if you could tell a robot to clean your room, make your favourite sandwich, or even play a song just by giving it a set of instructions. That's what coding is.

Coding is how we talk to computers and tell them what to do. Without coding, computers, tablets, and even video games wouldn't work. It's like writing a special language that computers understand.

Computers are powerful machines, but they don't think for themselves. They need clear instructions to follow. These instructions, called code, tell computers how to perform tasks, just like a recipe tells a chef how to cook a meal. If a step is missing or wrong, the computer won't know what to do, just like a cake wouldn't turn out right if you forgot to add sugar.

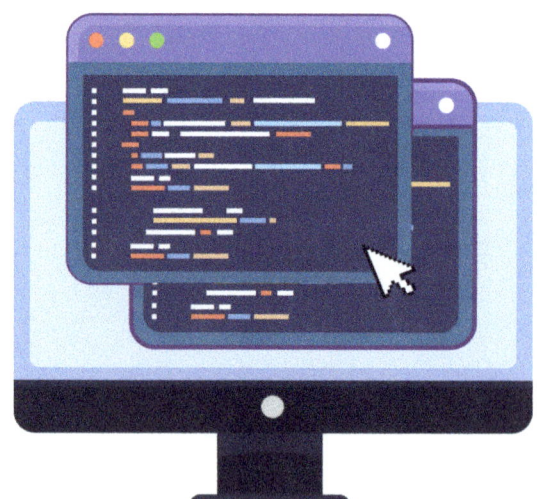

People use coding every day to create websites, design apps, and even control robots. Have you ever played a video game or used a school learning app? Someone had to write code to make that game work. Even traffic lights, space rockets, and medical machines use coding to run properly.

There are many different programming languages, just like there are different spoken languages such as English, Spanish, or Mandarin. Some popular coding languages include Python, JavaScript, and Scratch.

Each one has its own rules and is used for different things.

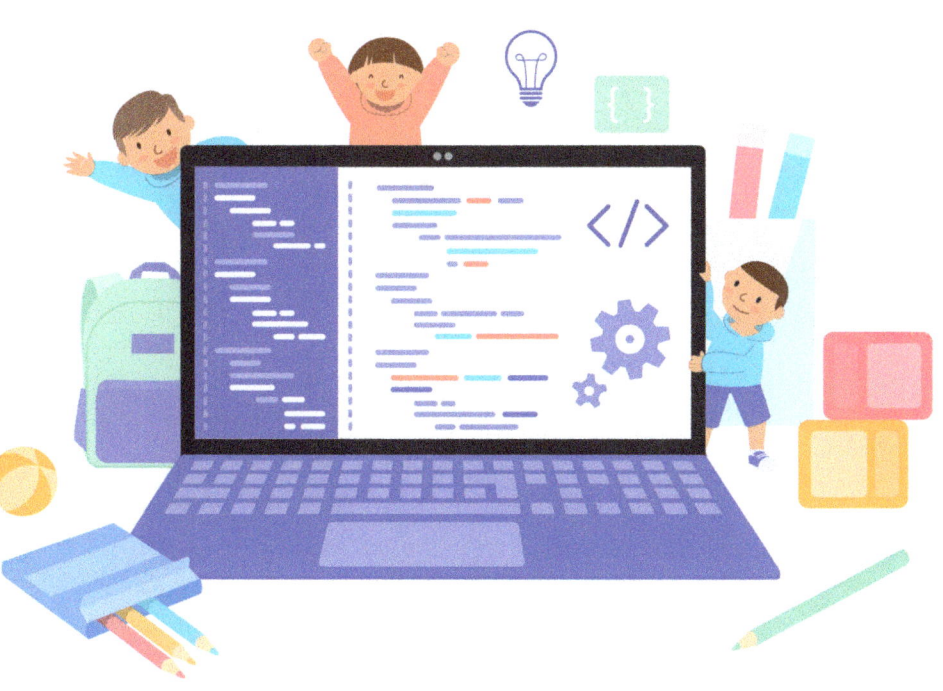

The best part? Anyone can learn to code, even you. Coding is like solving puzzles or playing with LEGO bricks. By learning to code, you can create your own games, design websites, and even build your own mini programs. In this book, you'll explore how coding works and why it's such an important skill for the future.

Code Your Name

Using a simple coding tool like Scratch or a pen and paper, try writing your name in a special "code." You can use numbers for letters (A=1, B=2, etc.) or create your own symbols for each letter. Can a friend decode it?

How do computers understand code?

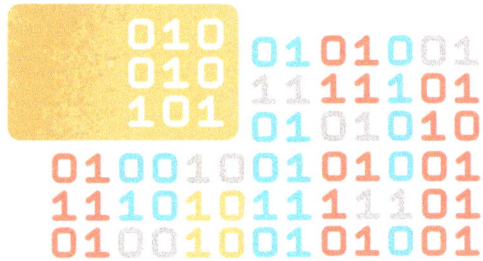

Computers may seem smart, but they actually don't understand human language like we do. Instead, they only understand binary code, a special way of writing information using just two numbers: 0 and 1.

Every video, game, or message on a computer is made up of thousands (or even millions) of these tiny 0s and 1s!

Binary code works like a secret language. Each letter, number, or picture on a screen is translated into a combination of 0s and 1s, which tell the computer what to do. For example, the letter "A" is written as 01000001 in binary. It might look confusing, but computers are really good at reading it super fast.

Because binary code is tricky for humans to write, programmers use programming languages to make coding easier. These languages help turn human instructions into a form that computers can understand. When you type a command in Python or Scratch, the computer converts it into binary code behind the scenes.

Have you ever used a remote control to change the channel or play a video? The buttons on the remote send binary signals to your TV, telling it what to do. That's just like how coding works, except instead of pressing buttons, coders write instructions in a programming language.

Learning how computers understand code helps us create better apps, games, and programs. Even though we don't have to write in binary, knowing that computers follow very precise instructions helps us become better coders.

In the next chapter, we'll explore different programming languages and what they're used for.

Coding Quiz

What language do computers understand?

a) English. b) Binary. c) Python.

What do the numbers 0 and 1 represent in binary code?

a) Colours. b) Letters and numbers c) Images

If you want to give instructions to a computer, what do you need to write first?

a) A story. b) Code. c) A book

Answer Key:

1) Binary 2) Letters and numbers 3) Code

What are programming languages?

Computers don't speak English, they need a special language to understand what we want them to do. This is where programming languages come in. Just like there are different spoken languages, there are many coding languages. Each one is made for a different job.

Python, for example, is great for creating apps and games, while JavaScript helps websites come to life. Scratch, on the other hand, is perfect for beginners because you can create games and animations using colourful blocks. It's like building with LEGO.

Some languages, like C++ or Java, are used to make big, complex projects like video games. Others, like HTML and CSS, help build the look and feel of websites. The best language to learn depends on what you want to create.

No matter which language you choose, the goal is the same: to communicate with the computer. When you learn how to code, you'll have the power to create your own projects, whether it's a game, a website, or something else entirely.

There's no one "best" programming language. The more you explore, the more you'll find the language that suits your interests and skills. So, which one will you try first? Let's dive into how you can start coding today.

Match the Language

Can you guess which coding language is used for what? Match the language to its purpose:

1. Python
2. Scratch
3. JavaScript
4. C++

A. Making websites interactive

B. Beginner-friendly, drag-and-drop coding

C. Building complex video games

D. Creating apps and simple games

(Answers: 1-D, 2-B, 3-A, 4-C)

How do coders write code?

Coders write step-by-step instructions called algorithms to tell a computer what to do. If the instructions are clear and correct, the program runs smoothly. But if there's a mistake, the program won't work as expected.

When writing code, programmers use something called **syntax**, a set of rules that must be followed for the code to work. Each programming language has its own syntax, just like different languages have different grammar rules. A tiny mistake, like missing a semicolon (;) or misspelling a command, can cause an error. That's why checking your code carefully is so important.

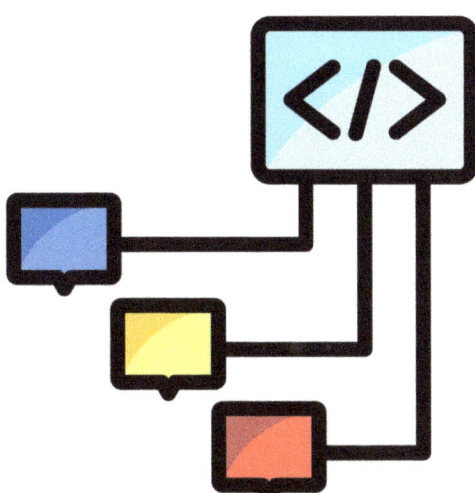

One of the most exciting parts of coding is **debugging**, fixing mistakes in your code. Even professional programmers make errors, but they use debugging to figure out what went wrong.

Sometimes, a missing letter or extra space can cause a program to crash. Coders learn to be patient and keep testing their code until it works.

Many coders write their code in a text editor or a special program called an IDE (Integrated Development Environment). These tools help organize and check the code, making it easier to find and fix errors. Some coding platforms, like Scratch, make coding even simpler by letting you snap commands together like puzzle pieces.

The best way to get better at coding is by practicing. Just like learning to play an instrument or ride a bike, coding takes time and effort. But once you get the hang of it, you can build your own games, websites, and even cool apps. The more you code, the better you'll become.

<u>Debugging Challenge</u>

Below is a simple line of code, but it has a mistake. Can you spot and fix it?

```python
print("Hello, my name is Alex)
```

(Hint: Check the quotation marks)

Answer : The mistake is that the closing quotation mark is missing. Once it is added, the code will work correctly.

What can you do with code?

Coding isn't just about computers, it's about creating amazing things. With code, you can design video games, build websites, and even control robots. Coders use their skills to solve problems, make life easier, and invent new technology.

Ever played Minecraft? The game is made using a programming language called Java. Many popular apps, like YouTube and Instagram, are built using different coding languages, too. Even smart assistants like Alexa and Siri use code to understand and respond to your voice.

Coding is also used in science and medicine. Doctors use computer programs to help diagnose diseases, and scientists use coding to study weather patterns and space exploration. NASA even uses coding to control Mars rovers and send rockets into space.

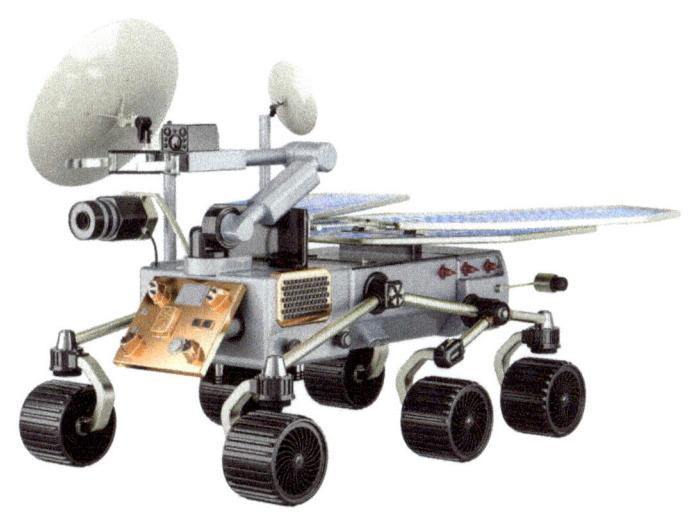

Have you ever heard of artificial intelligence (AI)?

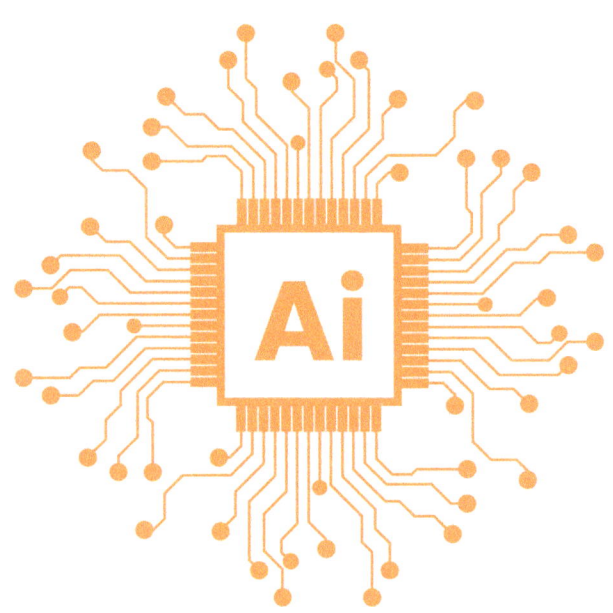

AI is a special type of coding that allows computers to learn and make decisions on their own. AI helps self-driving cars know when to stop, translates languages, and even suggests what video to watch next on YouTube.

The world runs on code, and learning how to code gives you superpowers to create and invent.

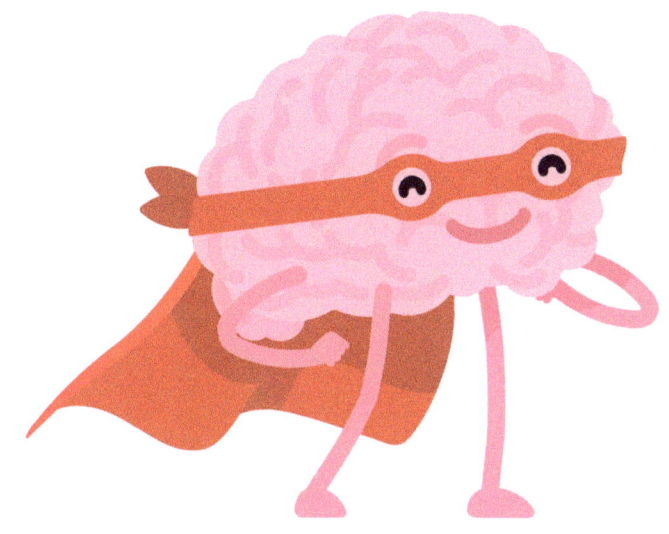

Whether you want to make your own app, design a robot, or solve real-world problems, coding is a skill that can help you do it all.

Future Coder Brainstorm

What would YOU create with code? Would it be a game, an app, a robot, or something brand new? Draw a picture or write a short description of your dream invention!

How do video games use coding?

Video games are fun to play, but have you ever wondered how they're made? Every jump, level, and special effect in a game is created using coding. Game developers use programming languages to bring their ideas to life, turning pixels into exciting adventures.

Every video game follows a set of rules written in code. For example, when you press the spacebar to make a character jump, the game follows a coded command that tells the character how high to go. If the code is wrong, the jump might not work at all.

Games also use something called game physics. This tells the game how objects should move and react. For example, in racing games, cars slow down when they hit the brakes. In platform games, characters fall back to the ground because of gravity. All of these effects are created with coding.

Many game developers use special programs called game engines to make coding easier. A game engine is like a toolbox full of pre-made coding tools that help developers build games faster.

Some popular game engines include Unity, Unreal Engine, and Scratch. Even beginner coders can use Scratch to create their own fun games.

If you've ever wanted to design your own game, learning to code is the first step! You can start by making simple games, like a maze game in Scratch or a quiz game in Python. With practice, you can build your own exciting adventures and maybe even create the next big game.

Make Your Own Game Idea

Think of a new video game idea. What's the goal of the game? What kind of characters, levels, or powers would it have? Draw a picture or write a short description of how your game would work.

How do websites and apps work?

Have you ever visited a website like Google or played a game on an app? Every website and app is powered by code. Coders use different programming languages to design, build, and make websites and apps work smoothly.

A website has two main parts: the front end and the back end. The front end is what you see and interact with, the buttons, pictures, and text. This part is created using languages like HTML, CSS, and JavaScript.

The back end is where all the data is stored and processed. It helps websites remember your login details or load new pages when you click a link.

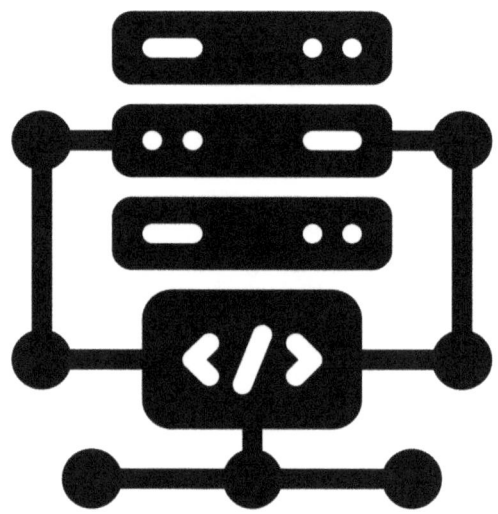

Apps work in a similar way. Whether it's a social media app, a weather app, or a game, coding makes everything possible. App developers use programming languages like Swift (for iPhones), Kotlin (for Android), and JavaScript (for web apps) to create interactive experiences.

One cool thing about websites and apps is that they connect to the internet. When you search for something on Google, code sends your question to a huge database, finds the best answer, and shows it on your screen in seconds.

Websites also use cookies, tiny pieces of code that remember your preferences, like your favourite theme or saved logins.

If you learn how to code, you can build your own website or app. Want to create a blog, an online shop, or a fun game? With a bit of coding knowledge, you can bring your ideas to life on the internet.

Design Your Own Website

Imagine you're making a website. What would it be about? A gaming site? A pet adoption page?

Draw or describe what your homepage would look like and what buttons it would have.

What is the future of coding?

Technology is always changing, and coding is helping to shape the future. Coders are working on exciting projects like self-driving cars, virtual reality, and space exploration. In the future, coding will be even more important in creating new inventions.

One of the biggest trends in coding today is artificial intelligence (AI). AI allows computers to learn and make smart decisions. You might have already seen AI in action, like when Netflix suggests movies or shows. Coders are teaching computers to recognise faces, translate languages, and even create art.

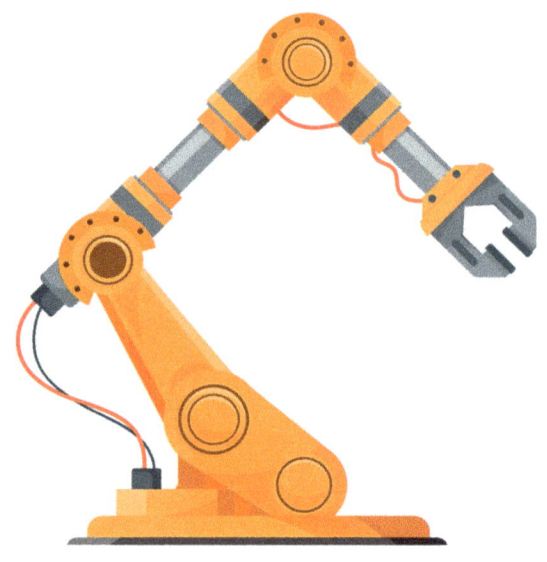

Another cool area is robotics. Robots are already being used in hospitals, factories, and even in space. Coding helps robots understand commands and complete tasks like delivering packages or performing surgery. In the future, we might even have robot assistants at home.

With so many exciting developments, the future of coding is full of possibilities. Maybe one day, YOU could be a coder who invents the next big thing!

Future Tech Predictions

Imagine it's the year 2050. What's one amazing invention that will change the world?

Draw your invention and give it a cool name. <u>Bonus</u>: Explain how it works in 3 sentences.

How can YOU start coding?

Now that you know all about coding, you might be wondering, how can you start coding today? The good news is, you don't need a fancy computer or expensive software to begin. There are plenty of free coding games and apps to help you learn.

One of the easiest ways to start coding is with block coding. Websites like Scratch let you create animations and games using colourful code blocks. This is a great way to understand how coding works before moving on to real programming languages.

If you want to try text-based coding, you can start with Python. Python is one of the easiest programming languages to learn, and you can use it to create simple programs, like a calculator or a quiz game. Other beginner-friendly languages include JavaScript and Swift.

The best way to get better at coding is by building projects. Try making a mini-game, designing a website, or even creating an animation. If you ever get stuck, there are tons of online tutorials and coding communities where you can ask for help.

Remember, every great coder started as a beginner. The key is to keep practicing, be curious, and have fun! Who knows? One day, you might become a software engineer, a game designer, or even an inventor of the next big tech breakthrough.

The first-ever computer programmer was a woman. Ada Lovelace, a mathematician in the 1800s, wrote the first algorithm designed for a machine, long before computers even existed. She imagined a future where machines could create music, art, and more, just by following instructions. Sounds a lot like today's coding, right?

Glossary

- **Code** – Instructions given to a computer to make it do something.

- **Programming Language** – A special language used by coders to talk to computers.

- **Python** – A beginner-friendly programming language used for many purposes.

- **JavaScript** – A programming language used for creating interactive websites.

- **C++** - A programming language used for creating high-performance programs like video games.

- **HTML** – A language used to structure websites.
- **CSS** – A language used to style and design websites.
- **Scratch** – A simple programming language used for creating games and animations.
- **Artificial Intelligence (AI)** – The creation of smart machines or computers that can think, learn, and solve problems, much like humans do.
- **Pixel** - A pixel (short for picture element) is the smallest unit of a digital image or display. Think of it like a tiny dot that, when combined with millions of others, creates the images you see on screens.

Loved learning about Coding?
Discover other titles in the Big Questions Series
Keep asking Big Questions Little Geniuses!

<CODE/>

www.ingramcontent.com/pod-product-compliance
Lightning Source LLC
Chambersburg PA
CBHW051603010526
44118CB00023B/2799